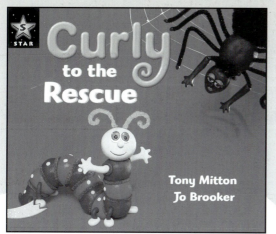

Walkthrough

This is

Can you remember the other Curly stories you have read?

Let's read the title: 'Curly to the Rescue'.

Who else is in the picture?

Do you think Spider is a nice character?

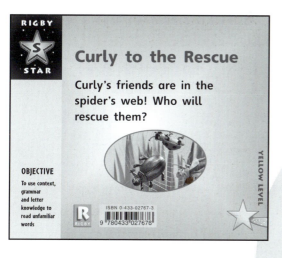

Curly to the Rescue

Curly's friends are in the spider's web! Who will rescue them?

OBJECTIVE

To use context, grammar and letter knowledge to read unfamiliar words

ISBN 0-433-02767-3

9 780433 027676

YELLOW LEVEL

Walkthrough

Let's read the blurb together.

What will the spider do to Curly's friends?

Curly to the Rescue

Tony Mitton
Illustrated by Jo Brooker
Photographed by Keith Lillis

Walkthrough

Let's read the title together: 'Curly to the Rescue'.

Which character can we see in this picture?

What do spiders like to eat? How do they catch their food?

Jo Brooker made the plasticine models and Keith Lillis took the photographs of them.

Walkthrough

What is the spider saying to the ladybird?

What do you think she is trying to do?

Point out alliteration in 'little ladybird.'

What will happen if the ladybird goes up to see the spider?

"Come up, little ladybird,"
said the spider.
"Come up and see me."

2

 **Observe and Prompt**

Observe one-to-one correspondence, particularly on two- and three-syllable words, e.g. 'little', 'ladybird'.

If a child has difficulty reading 'ladybird', ask the child to look for words within words and to check the picture.

Walkthrough

Who has come along? What colour is
the grasshopper? (*green*)

Point out alliteration and 'gr' letter cluster in
'green grasshopper'.

Will the spider want to catch him in her web?

What will she call out to him?

"Come up, green grasshopper,"
said the spider.
"Come up and see me."

4

Observe and Prompt

Check the children can read high frequency word 'come'.

Check they are able to segment and blend 'gr' and 'sp'.

What kind of creature is this? Is it little or big?

What will the spider say?

Who is trapped in the spider's web now?

What will happen to them?

"Come up, big beetle,"
said the spider.
"Come up and see me."

6

👁 Observe and Prompt

If a child omits 'big', remind him/her of the pattern of the text so far (alliterative phrases).

Ask the child to think of a word that would describe the beetle and which begins with 'b'.

If the child says 'blue', praise him/her for looking at the picture and say that 'blue' would make sense, but point out that the word is 'big'.

7

How is the spider feeling now that she has caught the creatures?

How can you tell she is pleased?

What might she be thinking?

The spider smiled.
"Hee hee!" she said.
"Now I will eat the ladybird
and the grasshopper and
the beetle for my tea."

8

Observe and Prompt

If a child has difficulty with 'ladybird', 'grasshopper' and 'beetle', return to previous pages and ask him/her to tell you who came to see the spider. Prompt child to use initial letter cues and words within words.

Walkthrough

Who came along? Where might the spider
have gone?

What are the other creatures calling out to him?

What do you think Curly is thinking?

Along came Curly.
"**Help!**" said the ladybird.
"**Help!**" said the grasshopper.
"**Help! Help!**" said the beetle.
"**The spider is going to eat us!**"

10

Observe and Prompt

Check the children are reading the bold words with
appropriate emphasis.

11

Walkthrough

Curly goes to look for help. Who does he see?

What does Curly tell the snail?

What do you think they will do?

Curly saw the snail.
"Help!" he said.
"The spider is going to eat
the ladybird and the
grasshopper and the beetle!"

12

Observe and Prompt

Check the children have noticed the speech marks and read with appropriate expression and intonation.

Walkthrough

What did Curly and the snail do to the web?

Did the plan work?

What will happen next?

Curly and the snail
pulled on the web.
Down came the web!

14

👁 Observe and Prompt

If a child has difficulty reading 'pulled', ask him/her to notice the
'ed' ending and then to re-read the word.

Observe appropriate expression is used for the last line.

15

Walkthrough

What do you think the creatures said when Curly set them free?

What did they do after they got free from the web?

What would you have done?

"Hurray!" said the ladybird and the grasshopper and the beetle. They all ran away.

16

👁 Observe and Prompt

Observe the children read with phrasing and fluency appropriate to the speech marks. Prompt by modelling the pause after 'Hurray!'

If a child reads 'run' instead of 'ran', prompt him/her to look at the middle letter of the word.